Travelling

Tales

the hourglass

Travelling Tales

the hourglass

stories and poems by
the *Redolant Writers*

Andrew Barclay

Elizabeth Jane

Ron Thomas

Matt Revert

REDOLANT
WRITERS

Travelling Tales
the hourglass

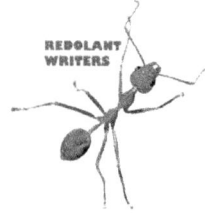

The Redolant Writers
Elizabeth Jane
Matt Revert
Ron Thomas
Andrew Barclay
Published by Redolant Writers

Author's note:
All characters in this anthology are inventions. The events described are all products of our imagingation.

Project editor: Andrew Barclay
Proof reading: Redolant Writers and Helen Reid
Cover design: Spatchcock
Images by: Andrew Barclay, Ron Thomas, Spatchcock, Iain Barclay

Redolant Writers
66 Torry Hill Road, Upwey, Victoria, 3158
Australia

National Library of Australia Cataloguing -in-Publication data:

Redolant Writers.
Travelling tales : the hourglass / by the Redolant Writers.

ISBN 9780987065100 (pbk.)

Redolant Writers

A823.4

Typeset in 11/14 pt Adobe Garamond Pro

Contributors

Elizabeth Jane

Travel is all about homecoming. My husband and I, have lived and worked in Fiji, visited New Zealand, and travelled in other Pacific countries. We have also enjoyed countless holidays on Australian soil. But my biggest journey was returning to my childhood 'home,' as an adult, in my early forties. As the aeroplane circled over Heathrow airport, I looked out over rows and rows of little brown houses. Seeing fields and meadows, in the distance, imagining owls, badgers and hedgehogs, and wondering, just wondering, how this was all going to feel.

Face pressed against the glass, I felt a deep jolt as the plane wheels hit the tarmac, and the salty sting of tears. Not silent tears. Great big chest wracking sobs. I was shocked to find myself thinking: If I die now, it doesn't matter, I'm here. I loved that holiday, not so much the icons, but the everyday things. Seeing the church where my parents married, the first home they lived in, meeting strangers who were family, jogging along the banks of the Thames. But strangest of all was coming back home to Melbourne, and finding I also belonged here.

Travelling Tales

Matt Revert

Travel doesn't exist. We move around a world in stasis. There is movement and there is stasis. We may momentarily leave the drudgeries of our own little lives to experience the drudgeries others experience in an environment different from our own, but that is all. Eliciting joy from your own environmental displacement requires the stasis of those in the environment you move to.

The world is a house with myriad rooms – most of which we'll never explore. We find comfort in our own room and have a hard time accepting visitors. When we burst into the room of another under the guise of 'travel', we are invaders. We are telling the owners of the room that we wish to absorb their room as a 'traveller' before heading back to our own safety – photos in tow to remind us (but mostly others) that we left our room for a while.

Travel is mere braggadocio, the exploitation of another's stasis. But this is okay. It's great for the economy. It gives you a story to tell. We all want stories, even if no one really wants to hear them.

What I'll never understand, is why we're so eager to explore the rooms of others before we even bother exploring our own.

Ron Thomas

Travel is twelve anus clenching hours on a Java bus. Travel is gatecrashing a five star bar of a luxury Vietnamese hotel to be serenaded by a torch singer and a pianist for the price of a cup of coffee. Travel is swaying woozily, almost as sick as your partner, in an outback Turkish 'hospital' with blood stained sheets, urine on the floors, cats and a stray vagrant passing through - and living to tell the tale. Travel is watching leaping pods of endangered Irrawaddy dolphins in the Mekong in Southern Laos.

Travel is life on fast forward. Travel is surfing the world. Travel is ideal life: freedom, spontaneity and constant learning - everything I adore.

the Hourglass

Andrew Barclay

Travel is an affair of the heart. It takes you to the most unexpected places.

It is arriving in England after a long flight and immediately calling a jumper a pully (pullover).

On a plane back from Europe the QANTAS steward leans across the back of the seat and says, 'What do youse want from the bar?'

After a trip to Ireland with its many shades of green, thoughts of ' what am I doing back home?' I drive the backblocks of regional Australia to Perth. I fall in love with Australia again, and its silvery-grey dusty green.

It is seeing the Centre around Alice Springs. The deep reds, burning blue sky and the hardy bush. Stellar stars. Solvent Dreamtime myths.

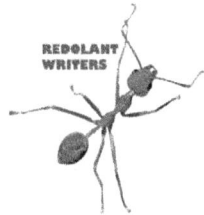

REDOLANT
WRITERS

Acknowledgements

I need to thank:

All the writers of *Travelling Tales*, Elizabeth Jane, Matt Revert and Ron Thomas. Our whole is stronger than the unit parts. I thank them for the faith they have put into the project.

Also Euan Mitchell and other inspiring teachers at Box Hill Institute who have made this possible. Nadine Creswell-Myatt, who has always given me her support. Tim Richards for his excellence in short stories.

Euan as the teacher of Professional Publishing gave patient guidance, sharing his exptertise in the publishing process and the InDesign software.

Paula for her inspiration in encouraging me to write. Mel and Lloyd who have helped me to continue. To my many supportive friends.

It is not everyday that an opporunity like this comes along, to create magic. I have tried my best to take advantage of the opportunity.

Andrew Barclay, Editor

Contents

Elizabeth
Jane

Biography

When Elizabeth Jane isn't writing, she works as a librarian, facilitates Balwyn Writers, and blogs at: *http:hannercymraes. blogspot.com.*

In 2007, an early draft of her historical novel, *Chrysalis,* was short listed for a HarperCollins Varuna manuscript development award. In 2008, it won an academic award.

In 2009, her short-story, *Beyond the Blackout Curtain*, won the Bristol Short Story Prize.

She is thrilled to be included in this volume of *Travelling Tales*.

When Neil Armstrong walked on the moon

by Elizabeth Jane

I had clear memories of the day Diana died. A friend called me with the news. I recalled the three shots ending John Lennon's life too, and the fall of Saigon. But I couldn't remember the Moon Walk, though I was forty five years of age, and it bothered me.

My husband Andrew remembered it clearly.

'It was the middle of the night,' he said. 'I watched it in my pyjamas.'

'That's funny, The Age says it was televised at 12:50 AEST.' I did a quick finger count. 'That's just past noon.'

Andrew peered at the newsprint. 'That can't be right. I remember the fuzzy black and white image.'

'Well according to this,' I stabbed the page. 'You watched it in the General Purpose Room at Hawthorndene Primary School.'

I didn't know why I was being so smug. He had a half memory, a strange jumble of TV experience. He'd probably seen the Moon Walk and simply confused it with another dressing-gown event, whereas I couldn't remember it, at all. No memory pinning me to the earth like gravity, no axis point from which to explore this moment of shared humanity — only a strange black hole in my understanding.

I would have been five years old at the time. The catechism of my family history says I came to Australia at the age of four and a half. That means I would have been in Geelong on July 21st 1969.

Closing my eyes, I could still see the pink fibro-cement house we rented in Herne Hill, near the cement works. The elephant climbing frame at Eastern Beach. The hill we rolled down, until we felt giddy and sick.

But I couldn't remember that 'one small step,' no matter how I tried. Neither could I remember the exact date we emigrated. For some reason, that too was also absent from my cache of childhood memories. Though, I couldn't think why. It was the AD of my childhood, the beginning and end of everything.

Aunty Jean cried at the airport. Mum was horribly sick. My brother Ian walked up and down the aisle of the Boeing 747, even at that age unable to keep still. Darwin airport had high ceiling fans, I remembered that clearly. Sometimes, when I lay awake at night, I could still hear them spinning, along with the low murmur of the airport lounge, and the gaunt soldiers returning from Vietnam. The memories are black and white, but clear, like an old school film strip — except the Moon Landing.

I decided to ring Mum.

'Hey Mum,' I asked. 'What date did we emigrate?'

'We left the 31st of August, 1969,' she said. It was a bank holiday. You were four and a half years of age.'

'Oh,' I said. 'That's strange. Then, I must have been in England for the Moon Landing?'

'Yes, dear, you were.'

I had a strange kaleidoscope feeling, at this point, my identity breaking up and shifting. At school I had started compositions with the words. 'I wasn't born in Australia. My family emigrated from the UK when I was four and a half years of age.' I met and married my husband on that sound basis. Later, when my own children reached that significant milestone, I watched them walk through the kindergarten gate, and thought: it happened when I was just this age. In my professional life, I have spoken in public, done interviews, all with the same absolute assurance.

Now it was being taken away from me

'But, Mum,' I said, 'I would have been five years of age on 21st of July, 1969.'

Silence on the end of the line.

I did a quick finger count. 'Are you sure you've got the date right? Mum, can you hear me?'

'I might be seventy two, Elizabeth. But I know when we emigrated.'

I did another count, slower this time. Maths had never been my strength. But I knew I was born on July 3rd 1964. I had seen the birth certificate. I also knew that nine take away four equalled five. That made me five years of age the day Neil Armstrong walked on the moon. It would have been 3:50 am on July 21st, GMT, and I would have been tucked up in bed.

No wonder I didn't remember the event. I was sound asleep. Mum and Dad were preparing to emigrate, selling furniture and packing boxes. About to embark upon their own momentous journey, leaving home, family, friends, and flying to the other side of the world. Henceforth to communicate with loved ones by infrequent letters and breathless three minute phone calls. The Moon Walk would barely have crossed their minds. Let alone an insignificant detail such as their daughter's age.

But it was significant — a new disturbing cold sweat sort of knowledge, that needed to be shared with the whole family. I wasn't sure how they'd feel on hearing the news, whether they would take a completely different view of me. Perhaps it would be like the day they found out Father Christmas wasn't real. They would have a deep biting sense of disillusionment: so, she lied. Nevertheless, the facts must be faced. They needed to understand the flimsy fabric from which our family myth had been woven. I took a deep breath, and announced it over a dinner of roast beef.

'I found out something important today.'

No response.

'About my family emigrating.'

'Yes, you were four and half years old, you've told us already.'

'Er, well that's the thing. I might have got it wrong.'

'No, don't tell me,' my son looked up from his plate. 'You are actually from Japan?'

'Don't joke,' I heard a wobble in my voice. 'This is serious.'

'Tell us,' my husband said, taking my hand.

'Well it seems I wasn't four and a half, at all.' I swallowed. 'I know I always told you I was, and I didn't mean to lie. But I rang Mum today, you know about the Moon Walk and it seems I was actually five years of age when we emigrated.'

'Four and a half, five,' my son shrugged. 'It's all pretty close.'

'Yes,' my daughter said. 'It makes no difference really.'

I looked down at the table, swift tears salting my eyes. They didn't care. It was just a story to them, something odd Mum kept repeating. It had no bearing on their present, or their future reality. They had their own calendar of half remembered experience, their own hoard of fractured images they'd have to reconcile at mid-life.

But it mattered to me — I was five years old when we emigrated, yes five, do you hear me? I wasn't sure why it had taken me forty years to work it out, or how it would alter my steps going forward. Only that it was significant.

I looked up at Andrew.

He squeezed my hand. 'So, you were in bed when Neil Armstrong walked on the moon.'

'Yes,' I smiled. 'Fast asleep.'

REDOLANT
WRITERS

Summer Sense

The smell is the thing at the beach, isn't it?
Not the stiff breeze or the colour of the sea
(Though those things are lovely)
Not the sand or rocks or the shells crunching underfoot
It is the smell pickled and tangy
The faint musty odour of mutton-birds nesting
A trinity of seaweed, salt and sun-cream
The smell, yes, and the sounds …
(The forgotten senses)
Of gulls wheeling and calling
The high distant cries of children playing
The swash of waves tumbling onto the beach
Scent and sound — sensual, subtle, subliminal
There when you close your eyes
Present on waking
Their message is clear as speech
It is summer in Australia
I am at the beach

by Elizabeth Jane

Image by Andrew Barclay

Matthew
Revert

Biography

Hailing from Melbourne, Australia, Matthew Revert is the washed up flotsam of the absurdist writing world.

Acknowledged by few and enjoyed by less, his fiction has been described as 'definitely written to some extent'.

His first book, *A Million Versions of Right* was released in July 2009 by LegumeMan Books. The overwhelming majority of people who have read this book have admitted to doing so.

In 2011 he wrote *The Tumours Made Me Interesting*.

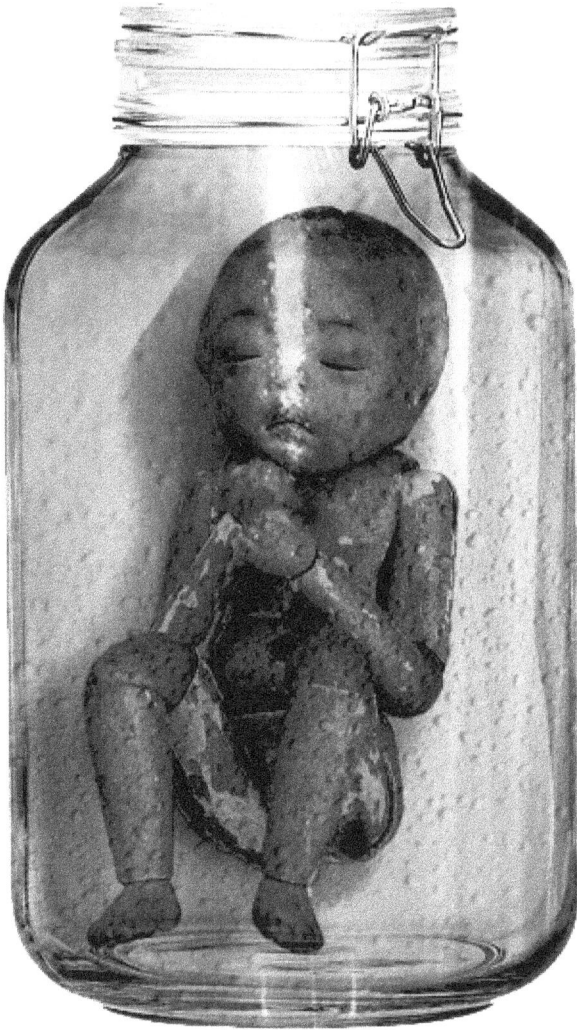

Image by Spatchcock

Vinegar Baby

By Matthew Revert

I was placed in an empty vinegar bottle shortly after my birth and left there to grow. My father, a doorknob named Blake, placed me on the mantle and blew me kisses from his favourite armchair each night before bed. His kisses, loving as they were, would simply splash against my bottle and drizzle downward. Some nights, I frenetically licked at my bottle walls, trying desperately to taste the slightest inkling of my father's kiss.

My mother chose to stop growing when she was 14 and maintained a pubescent awkwardness that was endearing in its own special way. Each year, on my birthday, my mother would cradle the bottle, with me inside. She would rock me backward and forward, gentle as the breeze from a silent fart. Then, for the most fleeting moment, she would remove the lid to my bottle and tickle me with a string of rose-scented drool. In these moments, I became infused with promise and insatiable desire.

On my 18th birthday, I found the inner strength to discuss travel with my parents. I wanted out. They discussed the matter in whispered tones while stopping every so often to look at their watches. It seemed unlikely that I'd ever be granted access to the outside world, but I had to try. Rather than immediately succumb to my desire, they performed a ukulele concerto.

I was left to stew in my bottle for many weeks after my initial request, which of course did little to buoy my optimism. But then, like a disco crotch grab, I was removed from the mantle and passed into the waiting hands of a milkman. Still ensconced within my bottle, I was placed into a crate, containing many similar bottles. These bottles were inhabited only by milk.

The milkman took me away. In the back of his truck, I watched a world I'd never known pass me by in a blur of confusion. It was terrifying and exhilarating in equal measure. I longed to remove the lid of my bottle and feel the breeze of freedom flood me. I longed to interact with people I'd never met. For perhaps the first time, I wanted to smash my way out of the vinegar bottle.

The milkman's truck was attacked by enormous crows, each the side of a modest cottage. The truck swerved left and right before skidding off the road entirely and kissing a tree. Through plumes of filthy engine-born smoke, the crows pecked and clawed at the bottles, knocking me about and inspiring nausea. A leathery talon clamped around my bottle and carried me away.

The world below me grew smaller and smaller until it resembled a rotten petrii dish. The crows muttered to one another in mysterious croaks. The higher we ascended, the darker the sky became. Chills vibrated through my body like broken speakers. A pocked sphere, resembling a very small moon, came into focus. As we approached, a very comfortable warmth started to envelop me, painting condensation on my ravaged bottle.

We touched down on the mini moon, my bottle rolling gently on the dusty surface. Exhaustion filled me to the brim and I closed me eyes. I began to pine for the safety of my mantle. I missed my parents. I missed my unsatisfying comfort. Tears pushed their way through my closed eyelids and began to fill the bottle.

I had been asleep for some time and awoke bobbing up and down in my tear-filled bottle. The crows surrounded me with wings spread, turning my world to black. Their beaks hung open ever so slightly. Together they hummed in a rich baritone that shook the alien earth beneath me. I tried covering my ears, but it only seemed to make the sound louder and more menacing. A chilling crack began to form and spread around my bottle. I curled into a foetal ball at the bottle's base, willing the situation to vanish.

the Hourglass

The shattering sounds of horrible freedom engulfed me. I felt shards of my bottle pelt me. I kept my eyes wrenched shut, unwilling and unable to open them. The bottle had been all I'd known. I simply couldn't fathom existence without it.

The first post-bottle experience to ravage me was the air. It clung to me like the desperate tongues of elderly cunnilingus. I had never felt anything more wretched. My unaccustomed skin began to dry and flake from my body and curl from its origin in a blizzard of dead me. The crows tried protecting themselves with their wings, but the drier my skin flakes became, the more dangerous they were. Like powdered razors, they tore through the crows until little more than avian blood smears remained.

New, slightly more resilient, skin spread across my pink body. I stared out at the uniform blackness of the sky, swallowing the wind and passing it out my backside. I was thoroughly alone, pining for my home… for my parents. The wind passing through me propelled me forward. The more wind I swallowed, the more propulsion I achieved. I lifted from the ground and moved through the air, slowly escaping the alien environs of the tiny planet.

The space air thickened into embryonic jelly, which I swam through with frog-like elegance. But the air continued to thicken, making my continued passage more problematic. I slowly passed other travellers, trapped in stasis, unable to move, frozen in perpetuity. Having capitulated to the struggle, they looked peaceful. Their closed eyes formed content smiles. I was at once struck by the singular notion that capitulating to the struggle is the only true way to avoid struggle completely.

My arms grew weary. Every muscle burned. Continuing forward promised me nothing so I stopped. My eyes gently fell shut, forming the same ocular smiles as my fellow travellers. Like them, I was a traveller no more. I wanted for nothing, nor did I miss anything.

REDOLANT
WRITERS

13

Ron
Thomas

Biography

Ron has taught Literature, English and Drama in Government schools for 35 years including directing about 20 musicals. He has been the Gifted and Talented Students Coordinator at Wantirna College.

As a freelance journalist he has had articles published in *The Sunday Age*, *The Advertiser* and *The National Senior*.

Writing, reading, travel and public speaking are the motifs which run through his life.

He has studied the CELTA ESL program so as to teach English overseas.

Ron is now concentrating on his debating and public speaking training business *Speak With Power*.

Scooter madness
image by Ron Thomas

To Tour or not to tour

By Ron Thomas

Approaching 60? Semi–retired? Or with Long service leave?
A bit of superannuation? Or an annuity? But still with a spark of adventure?

You have the means and the time to travel. But can't face lugging a back pack. Or squatting among the chickens in the dirt floor lean-to restaurant. Yet at the same time repelled by the five-star, sanitised, guided tour for the expensive, the artificial and the well trodden.

Well, you don't have to choose – you can have the best of both worlds. You can travel independently with comfort, safety and ease to exotic places like Vietnam, Cambodia and Laos.

*

I am over 55. With my partner I have travelled independently to lesser known South East Asia.

We had backpacked the world in our youth, now the kids had finally finished High School and could drive. We could leave them the house and the dog to look after – and resume our travels.

But how to do it? My wife's back wasn't up to a backpack any more. Were we compelled to take a tour?

We went to one of the more adventurous tours information nights. The slides were mostly of the, admittedly swish, accommodation. There was great emphasis upon 'our guides'. The people around us seemed pleasant enough but we felt there was more sausage than sizzle. The 'exclusive' cooking classes sounded great but we later found out they were far from exclusive – available everywhere and much, much cheaper purchased in Hoi An, Vietnam.

What to do? We had nine weeks and three countries to see so we decided we'd freelance it.

Travelling independently has turned out so easy. The sum of negative experiences have been: an unscheduled night in Ha Tien due to a fire on a ferry (it happens to tours too), a hundred minute wait for a bus connection at the Don Kong ferry terminal in southern Laos – it could have been the Belgrave line! And a couple of days tummy trouble quickly fixed by the impressively named Office Medicale de l'Ambassador de France in Vientiane. Again, tours are not immune either.

*

So how do you do it?

Essential number-one – get a guide book, one for each country but, check that it is up to date.

Lonely Planet is excellent but a few words of caution.

They occasionally get things wrong. As they admit, things change. The un-missable gastronomic experience of Ho Chi Minh City, Quan Na Gnoc, has moved a block away. Which is where the internet comes in, but more on that later.

There are usually more and better options since printing. Laos for example had newer and better buses than claimed. These countries are developing at a furious pace. When we discovered the guesthouse we had booked at Vang Vieng, Laos was full, they found us a better one next door for the same price that had just been built. Some canny places advertise, 'We are not in 'Lonely Planet' but we soon will be!'

The budget and youth end is better catered for than other demographics. So if you want to do more than drink you may have to seek out Art and other entertainments yourself. Again use the internet, which is usually free at most guest houses or 20 cents an hour at the ubiquitous internet cafes. Free Wifi is everywhere (if you take a laptop).

the Hourglass

*

Essential number two – Get a local SIM card for your mobile phone.

These are really cheap and allow you to ring home to check if the kids have starved the dog for a fraction of the cost of global roaming. The drawback though is they can ring you about things you are trying to forget. Turn it off and pretend poor reception!

A local SIM means you can fool proof your trip. A day or two (more in peak times) before you move on, ring ahead and book your selected hotel from the guide book or the internet. This gives you the freedom tours can't. 'Love a place – stay another day' – Luang Prabang's easy to agree with motto. Hate a place, like Vang Vieng, a back packers' party paradise, everyone else's purgatory. Leave immediately.

Bonus: 90% of the time the guest house you book will meet the plane/ bus/boat eliminating transfer hassles – which is what tours do. Our Kampot, Cambodia, host rang us back when our bus was late to see where we were!

*

Essential number three. Don't be frightened. There is nothing to fear but fear itself.

Your guide book has lots of warnings – heed them – they are just common sense. But don't let them put you off or develop a distrust of the locals. I have been travelling for over two years and I have never been robbed, never been ripped off (more than a few dollars) and never missed a transport connection.

On the other hand, I have been chased down a Bangkok street by a restaurant owner desperate to return my airline ticket, passport and money I had left on the restaurant seat on the afternoon of my departure; had 100,000 dong notes rejected because they should have been 10,000; and been prevented from boarding the wrong transport on a number of occasions.

Even tuk–tuk drivers, after rejecting their advances, will give you advice. Even ask other people's guides your questions they are keen to show off their knowledge. Remember they are people just like us. Everyone, who isn't

19

trying to make money out of you, wants to help.

*

Four ways to easily avoid the hassles that tours claim to solve.

Firstly, arm yourself with knowledge. Get a reasonable idea of the prices to expect from your guide book. Our experience is that $20 per night in the book is really $25 a year later. Tuk-tuk prices are usually accurate. Use your guide book maps to figure the distance your hotel is from where you are, multiply by the per kilometre price and you have a ball park figure. *Tell them* that this is how much it should be. Walk away if they double it. They'll come down. If they walk away the last price was probably ok - so take it.

Secondly, remember every service will cost you, and worse, end up in a haggling hassle. Never take the first offer. Don't be rushed. Trundle your cases to the nearest cafe/restaurant. Have your partner mind the cases while you *suggest the price* to the hotel. Or if you don't have a hotel, check out the ones around you or even the touts' places - at your leisure. In Luang Prabang, the guide book's choice was distant, expensive and noisy. One we just walked into was on the riverfront, quiet and half the price for the same standard!

Thirdly, talk to other travellers. This is much harder on a tour, and not as necessary, so you remain quite insulated from one of the greatest joys of travel. I met so many Europeans in India it set up my trip to Europe. A Danish friend I made even lent me his car in Copenhagen. Paris Beach Hotel on Phu Quoc Island, Vietnam, (recommended by a random encounter) wasn't even in the book but it meant we got a room when all the book's listings were full.

Even better other travellers' disasters can be your saviour – 'Don't stay in central Vang Vieng, Laos unless you want old episodes of *Friends* blared at you and drunken stoned backpackers raging in the bedroom next door.'

Fourthly, talk to the locals. Your organised tour guide is an expert on the history and the culture but rarely as close to the struggle of real life as the local bloke you can pick up at Angkor Wat. Our guide, Ratanak, had lived on rice and fish sauce for 5 years to get his Guides Certificate! The trek leader to Mt Bokor, Kampot was the only living member of his family. The Khmer Rouge had a cuppa after shooting everyone but him and he was able to slip away into the jungle. He subsisted there for 2 years until the Vietnamese liberation which he then joined. So he could say with confidence, 'there are no land mines here – I know - because I cleared them.'

It's the emotional connection not the great photograph or dissertation that'll make your trip.

*

So independent or organised?

If you do it yourself you will have to spend time on organisation. However, it's time well spent. We left internal airfares until we were over there and saved 40%. We left visas to Laos and Cambodia until the day before arrival and they were done in hours. Competition is so fierce that in many places like Luang Prabang, at night (when there's little to do) after a great meal at Tamarind, of course, you can stroll from agent to agent looking for the best deals up to 10 pm! We were a little dubious but everything worked.

If you do it yourself your experience can actually be richer. In Na Trang, and most places in Vietnam, you can go anywhere in a city by taxi for 2 or 3 dollars. You can book guest houses that have free bicycles – a great way to see Hoi An. In Hue, the Emperors' tombs and pagodas can easily be done in a day on motor scooter – although you'd be brave to do this in Hanoi or Ho Chi Minh City. If you get really adventurous you could organise your own border crossing from Kampot, Cambodia, to Phu Quoc, Vietnam. There are no buses, so you must hire a tuk tuk – a lovely leisurely way to cruise through rural Cambodia, then change to three motorbikes, one for each of you and one for the luggage, as tuk tuks are not allowed to cross.

*

Tours emphasise the risk of doing it yourself but few people factor in the risks of doing a tour.

Risk one: the company you keep. A tour guide we met (from a highly popular Australian Tour Company), admitted she had one tour that was all men. They had decided to take on a tour to meet women. Another tour we met had one American and 15 Aussies – imagine it the other way round!

Risk two: the Guide. We shared a guest house with a tour for two days (ironically the *Lonely Planet* recommendation) in the 4,000 islands in the Mekong of Southern Laos . The guide never shut up. Two or three weeks of it would have been murder.

Risk three: the weakest link. This can be the fatty, the fussy, the freaked out or any other extreme of human behaviour.

*

Put it this way, to travel independently you must have at least a minimum level of competence.

*

So - *To Tour or not to tour?*

In our minds, whilst we are fit, there is no question. So why not join the thousands of people your age travelling independently. We almost outnumber the young back packers already.

Image by Ron Thomas

In the Buffet at the Station
Eperney 8.30 am Sunday

Rock around the clock

Scratches from the jukebox
The man with the too red face
Stands at the bar of his life
And sips a Sunday morning beer
With painstaking slowness

A train of Toute Grande Vitesse
Hums through the periphery of vision – and
consciousness.

Les vendages, fingers red-as-grapes,
Drink their backaches as coffee
The tobacco in the young girl's 'rollie'
Is the eye of the vortex
Her whole being spirals about.
The black man sits – unsure, quiet.

The barmaid, still pretty, still laughing -
Not yet broken –
Feels the tug, awaits the pull,
Of the rough waters of the hard life
That will ultimately engulf her.
The work bent men spar with her
In smiling complicity
of their mutual fate.

by Ron Thomas

Unpacking the mental backpack
Or
How do you capture the essence of 300 days of solo travel in just 500 words?

FLYING
Pressurised. Sanitised. Refrigerated. A trembling restaurant.
Scratched-perspex distortions of clouds and distant deserts.
A pleasant purgatory.
Reality, as hard as a bad landing, as inevitable as death.

FIRST STOP: Calcutta
She's a sick elephant: twitching, lurching – infected, her blood, long dark queues, snaking towards the Goddess of Information. Alas the Goddess has been atomised. Queue here for her sari? No. Here. Stations are her temple, (but there are others). Bureaucrats her keepers – 'I can show you her face – if you know the right rituals.'
Overburdened, leg-chained by her millions, India shuffles, marking time.

THIRD WORLD BUS
Night blind down anorexic roads
Dwarf-seated between a mountain of women and a mountain of livestock. Careering giddily through unknown near misses. I'm sick and liquid. Twelve anus-clenching hours - no stops.

the Hourglass

PARIS
Centre Pompidou. Voyez-vous La mime? Le cirque? La sculpture?
Bonnard peut-etre? La photographie?
Tout, s'il vous plait.
Lost exalted hours in a labyrinth of modern genius.

SHARING A VAN
Entombed in a Bedford van. Kiwi couple: Sandy 'My aunt has this great tea
set' and Dean 'I can't park on the dirt' Williams.
'Why can't you drive like Dean,' she whines.
Obligingly he sideswipes half the cars in Barcelona.
Tyres bulging, battery melting, fights and tears – stuff the money – piss off.

ONE NIGHT STAND
Travelling hard – last bed, gravel beneath a bridge.
Evening: café etudiant, my kiwi confreres debate rugby with the French over
the beat of a Scottish band and jug after jug of vin ordinaire.
'Ullo, I am Michelle.'
Black keys (my English), white (her French), play an unlikely harmony of
understanding.
My mates retire to a rain drenched night in the park, I to liquor logged love
in her bed.
Dawn: cursorily dumped, before her daughter awoke.

GREEK ISLAND
Amorgos. Tramping a dusty scar. Pushing through luminous sky.
Rock – thorn. Thorn – rock. Rock – rock.
Waterless. Manless. Treeless.
Then goat after tinkling goat.

FOOD
Morrocan loaves blisteringly hot. Plateau Geant de Crustaces, Place Clichy.
The red wine of Kortula. Raw sea urchin and smoked octopus.
Dom Perignon.
Noodles and vegetables haggled in the market,
clandestinely cooked in the gardens of Nice.
Haggis. Paella.
A bottle of water on a Turkish bus.

EURAIL
First class. Eurail pass.
Automoton Austrians – not a second late.
Guten Nacht Hamburg, bon matin Paris.
Buon viagio. Kalo Taxidi.
Dutch author. Danish director.
My pack beside briefcases, boots by high-heels -
an unshaven frog among Princes.

NITTY GRITTY
Sewing the thread-bare sleeping sheet. Catching up ten days of the diary.
Washing the jeans in the shower. Learning "How much" in every new
language. Letters missed because your plans changed.
Waiting for money. Leaving a new friend – a little death.
Airports, bus stations: ferries that never arrive.
In a hotel bin, the sad stinking remnants of boots that have been through it
all.

BELFAST/LIVERPOOL FERRY
Cacophanous sea. Swells and troughs of sound.
Squalls and eddies of laughter.
Blasts of aggression. Steady pelting football argument.

Tribal chants and boot bangs against the cigarette machine.
All pitching, tossing into unconsciousness, as we slide towards Liverpool.
Marooned by the toilet, just beyond reach of the foaming Guinness carpet,
the red sleeping bag of a world-weary traveller
twitches sleeplessly.

HISTORY
Bullet holes in East German columns. Mohammed's forearm! Charleman's
chalice. Rothenberg Museum of Torture.
Dachau .... Dachau ....
Church of the Holy Sepulchre. Opium fields of the Kuo Min Tang.
Harvest in India. Disneyland? Buddhist chants with the Dalai Lama.
Iranian friends arrested on our bus.

FLIGHT HOME
Torn, worn and air-borne.
Smack back amidst the fat, crass and affluent
Reading "The Magus" quoting Eliot,
"And the end of all our exploring
Will be to arrive where we started
And to know the place for the first time."
The Mormon missionary beside me asks,
"What are Australians like?"

Home as inevitable as death.

by Ron Thomas

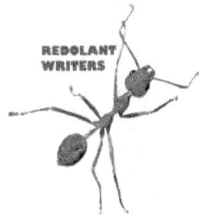

REDOLANT
WRITERS

Andrew Barclay

Biography

I was born under a corn stalk, roused by the Salvation Army's brass on Sunday mornings. Voluntarily deported from Britain to help make Australia a bright and wonderful land.

I am a librarian, writer, conversational philosopher, public speaker. Writing to me represents a window. If you don't frame it and open it you don't know what's inside.

I enjoy going to poetry readings. Poems are meant to be spoken. My first published poem appeared in *Avant* 2010 - I used the name Andrew James in honour of my father.

Travelling Tales is my attemtpt to put a personal slant on travel in a story telling style.

Old Man Storr

image by Andrew Barclay

Leaving Skye

by Andrew Barclay

Drizzle, sheep, cows in the mist. The rumbling road to Skye.

'Danny, what's your Dad like?' Alice asked. 'If he were like mine, I wouldn't bother to see him. Bastard'

'Dad's OK,' I replied,' I haven't seen him for a while. He left Mum in Melbourne, she was glad to see the back of him. He said he needed space. Skye! Couldn't get far enough away. Why Skye? I don't know. He likely wanted an excuse to be miserable. He's my Dad though, I want you to see him.'

*

I read in the guide, the *Skye Wanderer*, 'Do not whistle while on the island. It will bring you bad luck.'

Here from the Cuillin Mountains, over the sound to Raasay. There the people are strict in their observance of the Sabbath.

There's rain on the road and the light is low. Skye the Misty Isle, starfish mountains, the winged isle, an island of whispers.

I want you to like this island, with its magic.

31

'Do I look all right?' asked Alice.

'You look beautiful,' I replied. 'That red and yellow woolly looks good on you.'

'Look at you, you look like a black Hamlet, always serious,' teased Alice. 'I love your tight lips.'

'It's freezing up here.'

They had met on a bridge in Bath.

'I just had to find out who you were,' I said.

'I remember,' replied Alice. 'How we held hands. And that tangerine kiss.'

*

'There's a hostel by the waterfront,' I said. 'A friend in Liverpool told me about it. He came up here in the summer.'

From the hostel we could see the bridge to Kyle.

The *Skye Wanderer* described Skye Bridge as, now, free to cross. Once there were massive tolls that no-one paid. The locals preferred to swim across the sound rather than drive over the bridge.

'That bridge, like a dying coat hanger,' I thought. 'Like the one over to Phillip Island, only bigger. Easy to cross. Then you enter another world.'

I turned and walked to the nearby pub. I had to find my father's croft.

'How can I get to Cowcraig, Mr Banner's place?' I asked.

'It's near twenty minutes from here out of town. You'll never get there on foot,' replied the fearsome man at the bar. 'I'll take you out there in an hour. He is one of those dreighs living rough.'

Just another blow-in.

*

We could not believe the state of the house. The door was half off and the paintwork looked like potato peel.

'How does he survive the winter?' I asked.

'Get on with it Danny. It's cold out here. Let's get it done with.' urged

the Hourglass

Alice.

As we approached the croft we were met by a dog with teeth that looked like a dinosaur's. It was held to a tree-size post by double chains.

We didn't have to wait long before the croft door opened. A wild man appeared.

'Who is this drogbach at my door. Get thee gone!'

It was my dad, Michael.

He had changed his name to Michael Cuchullainn. He wanted the power of the ancient mighty Celtic warrior, who by legend was said to be a Lord of Skye. Michael had bought a fierce dog which he called Luther, after Cuchullainn's hound, Luath. Luther was Michael's show of power.

Michael's neighbours laughed at him to his face. 'Jumped up sassanach.' But they still feared him enough to go there armed with a heavy bat.

'Dad, is it you? Let us in. It's Danny, come to see you.'

'Who? I'm not expecting anyone,' his Dad bellowed.

'You should answer your phone. I know you've got one,' I replied. 'We've come a long way, pull your dog aside. We're coming in.'

If I'm anything I'm stubborn. If I want something, I'll keep at until I get it.

'Bloody strangers,' said Michael. 'Who's this then?' pointing at Alice.

'Dad, this is Alice. We're travelling together. I want you to meet her.'

'It's cruel that they keep sheep here,' said Alice. 'Out in all weathers. It's not right.'

Alice had looked after many animals who had suffered abuse from their insensitive owners. She felt cold for the sheep.

Michael glared at her, 'Some folk don't know what they're talking about.'

Alice's beauty disturbed him. She reminded him of his ex, stunning. But marriage had turned him bitter. Alice reminded him of his loss.

'Danny, you should tell your Alice she looks like a slut,' said Michael. He could see her bare legs. He'd pick on anything.

'Get out of it Dad,' I replied, 'and do something about that dog of yours. We've made a lot of effort to see you. I love Alice, we're together.'

*

Later Michael stirred. He had to concede something to his son.

33

'Danny, Alice, get up. I'll show you Old Man Storr, Master of the Cuillin mountains,' he said. 'A couple of hours and we'll be done.'

As they piled in the car Michael stopped to stare at Alice.

'Are you going to climb in thongs! You'll hurt yourself. You'll slip. It gets cold up there.'

'I'll be fine. Just look after yourself,' she snapped.

The path up the hill was slippery but Alice did not complain. She would not give in to crazy Michael.

When they got to the saddle Michael told his version of the Storr legend.

'This has been a special place since Neolithic times. Here, the gods ate and danced. The spirit of the mountains smiled on them. See those peaks? They are two brothers who broke the spirits' rules. They were turned to stone for their defiance.'

On the way down Alice slipped and twisted her ankle. As she clutched it, Michael just looked at her.

'Bloody idiot,' he muttered.

'Dad, I told you, lay off.'

You bastard, I can see you turned to stone.

We could not get away from Michael quick enough.

'Dad drive us back to Kyleakin,' I said, 'We have to get back to the hostel.'

Dad grumbled but obliged. 'I've had enough.'

The hostel was great.

'Come on Danny, let's get down to the lounge,' urged Alice.

I was more than happy to go.

'This is better. Noise, whisky and guitars. It's on.' I thought.

Failte, cheers.

*

'There's a group of us going to travel the island, are you coming?' smiled Marco. An offer too good to refuse.

We stopped at the stone bridge.

'This is the stream of dreams. Dip your face into the water and you'll have eternal youth,' said Marco.

I dipped my face into the icy, racing stream.

the Hourglass

I looked up at Alice.

I hope so.

The narrow road took us among the mossy hills.

'Come this way,' invited Marco. 'Fairy Glen, see what you think?'

Fairy Glen, a small valley with steep rising banks. At first it was hard to see anything special about it.

'Look to your right, there is the castle protecting the glen,' said Marco.

'There's the walls and the keep,' said Alice. 'Let's get up there and look from the top.'

'There's a snail shaped coil of rocks down there,' I said. 'Let's walk in and find the middle.'

How good it was to be together.

'No-one knows how long this place has been this way,' remarked Marco. 'They don't ask too many questions, else they'll offend the fairies.'

'This is the place for us,' said Alice, taken in by the peace.

*

We stopped at a broken castle overlooking the ocean.

'Duntulm Castle – for centuries the seat of the Macdonalds of the Isles,' declared Marco.

There was an inscription which read, 'The stone shall cry out of the wall and the beam out of the timber shall answer it - The prophesy of Habakkuk.'

The pain of life from the drawn sword.

'Dunvegan castle, the old seat of the Macleods of Macleod and still inhabited,' presented Marco.

Dr Johnson had visited and wrote, 'No man was naturally good, no more than a wolf.'

That's Dad for you.

'Are you happy you came?' I asked Alice.

'The island is fantastic,' she replied, 'I like the spirit. It is lived in, a hard place. And they believe in spirits too.'

*

Travelling Tales

That evening we took a skinny dip in the water outside the hostel.

'I dare you to do it!'

'Softie, you too.'

We emerged red-cold but emboldened.

*

'We'll have to try to see Dad one more time. Make him see sense,' I said.

'He'll have a go at me again, I know,' replied Alice. 'I don't want to.'

But I did not want to give my Dad up for dead yet.

'Please, for me – we won't be here again.'

'Well, OK. But I've nothing to say.'

We approached Dad's croft.

'Where's the dog?' Alice asked, hearing no sound.

'What's that by the door?' I asked.

'God, he's shot the dog!'

I pushed the door to, carefully. Dad lay flat on the floor, gun in his hand. Blotchy red face, bottles scattered.

He opened his eyes and saw me.

'Drop her or I'll shoot her,' he slurred.

*

At the post office in Portree we asked the postmistress the fastest way to leave the Island.

Flora the postmistress was a large woman. Alice observed her plaid Celtic cross in blue on her lapel.

'What's that cross on your dress?' she asked.

'It's a memory. My great grandmother helped Bonnie Prince Charlie escape from the island,' Flora replied.

He escaped just as we will.

'Take a fishing boat to Uist and make your way from there. Ask at the quay for Gordon, he'll help you,' continued Flora.

Failte – cheers and thank you

the Hourglass

*

The headwind was fresh as we sailed to Uist, Skye receding in the mist.
    I heard the words, *Sail bonny boat like a bird on a wing.*
    We're together

Bridge of ageless beauty

image by Andrew Barclay

Sunset Dreaming

by Andrew Barclay

The dream

Between the fingers of hope
Fact and fiction
Reality and dreams
Striving and love

The flow

One day I will ride a river
Take a boat to an exotic place
Find paper wings

Satisfaction

When right things complete
when they do.
I feel fulfilled.

Light

how quiet
silent sun
through the window
on my open page

the Hourglass

Child home

Child sight
Saxon hedged farms
Handkerchiefs past to present

Leaving home

tick tick tick tick
tick tick tick tick
tick tick tick
chair fireplace
cracking logs
watchful clock
charged silence

Return

The houses the same
The school gone
dismembered red brick shavings
bomb shelter long gone
street walk empty shell
The past is another country

my sunscreen
   my grain of sand

I have seen the sun fall
Uluru blood
red turning purple

butane blue paper pyre
surface slight
burnt gift to the gods

stiletto champagne celebrations among the cars
horseless Spring Carnival dancing
friend dervish dancing
hail rock tee shirt photos against the
silver-grey spiked spinifex
the scuffed red earth
and the deepening rock

Anangu chanting to Tjukuritja Waparitja
the lives of moment the spirit ancestor
defiantly home at the foot of the rock

I have seen the sun fall on Darwin
camera probing tree claws
sun's ink laser lighting
the Arafura sea

Sun fall at Broome the ultimate beach head?
and I the grain of sand

I have seen the sun fall on Darwin
camera probing tree claws
sun's ink laser lighting
the Arafura sea

Sun fall at Broome the ultimate beach head?
and I the grain of sand

Uluru sunset
image by Andrew Barclay

Guatemala

a play of light

your fan fold face

the Guatemalen night sun

your old man's life embrace

Image by Iain Barclay

Mekong sunset

image by Ron Thomas

tchau

www.ingramcontent.com/pod-product-compliance
Lightning Source LLC
Chambersburg PA
CBHW022343040426
42449CB00006B/692